Madness
and
Retribution

Madness

and

Retribution

Poems

Juliette Torrez

Manic D Press
San Francisco

Cover painting: Mark Ryden
Cover design: Scott Idleman/Blink

Library of Congress Cataloging-in-Publication Data

Torrez, Juliette, 1966-
Madness and retribution : poems / Juliette Torrez.
p. cm.
ISBN 0-916397-95-5 (trade pbk. original : alk. paper)
I. Title.
PS3570.O7385M33 2004
811'.54—dc22
2004008763

For James

Contents

ALBUQUERQUE

as i drive down albuquerque streets
edges of houses pop out of gray sky
undisguised by barren trees

twenty-three shades of brown
stucco painted to look like adobe
we're driving past, past the porches

where strings of red chile
hang there in welcome
how now brown town?

and it's good to be here
though when i'm gone
i don't miss you much

i even dogged you
albuquerque
because you are

a hard-hearted town
dressed in fake mud
being something you're not

personality split by two sides of the city
uptown and downtown,
the heights and the valley

split by businessmen
developing their property
you never had a good image of yourself

albuquerque
you don't love yourself the way
san francisco loves itself

the way seattle loves itself
the way santa fe loves itself
and i wonder what crime

stained these hills
that made you such a hard-hearted town
dressed in brown

ribboned in interstate asphalt
and a poisoned river
i'm fascinated by your sinister side

albuquerque
and pray you don't claim me
as a blood sacrifice

but when i come back
i see the way the sunset hits the sandias
and remember what it was

that i miss about this town
i see the morning light bright blue
the smell of cedar burning in the air

and remember what i miss
about this town
and when i go to the frontier restaurant

and ask for a green chile burger
they know exactly what it is
and they give it to me

and i remember
albuquerque
i love you i hate you

i'll always come back to you
the land of entrapment
a curse or a blessing

i don't know the answer
albuquerque
i just keep returning

CITY OF ANGELS

the city seems quiet
in the purple twilight

palm tree silhouette
middle of the night

but it isn't, he tells me
        right now someone is raping a woman

        right now someone is getting assaulted
        right now someone is getting their car stolen

        in this city it happens
        every 8 seconds

        i didn't even finish saying that
        before it's happened already again

        muggings, jackings, murders, larceny
        right now someone is coming home

        as a victim of burglary
        right now something is going down

but you know what
i love this town

it lets me do whatever i want

DALLAS

modern day city rich with oil
spread out like kingdom come

uptight dallas lets loose in deep ellum
picnic on the grassy knoll

cold chicken and clear pepsi
man in the condom shop

his left eye is skewed
i wonder if he sees me double

double almond latte
    honey, you must be from seattle

beautiful children go upstairs
to smoke

and talk about
last night's rave

he looks so good
hair tumbling down

    for a second, honey, you looked
    like my aunt grace, i say teasing

    that's okay, he replies, you dye
    your hair same color as my grandma

impersonal thistles
watch

our progress
through north texas

wildflowers whisper secrets
only i can hear

    stupid girl, happiness in your grasp
    thrown away for a summer adventure

madness is offered
as an explanation

DIFFERENT KIND OF PEOPLE POWER

sometime just recently
the world took a turn

hitched a motor to celebrity
to see how far it would go

british invasion in the home for old rockers
punk rock gods now corporate shills

image became everything
greed became justified

charles darwin economics
people trampled in the stampede

tower of babel flattened
the sixties became a selling point

anything slightly different was absorbed
by the marketing machine

and sold to the masses
d.e.a. agents cruising parking lots

of grateful dead shows but jerry is dead
and mandatory minimum is still

five years in federal prison
caring commodified

easily packaged in digestible servings
television is the magic filter

bringing everyone together
you don't even have to know your neighbors

I WANTED TO BE WONDER WOMAN

i wanted to be wonder woman
when i was younger
i wanted to kick ass
have the invisible plane and
a rich rewarding superhero life
outside of the public mundane

i wanted to believe in the constitution
and the bill of rights
i wanted to believe that
the military was necessary
that journalism was factual reporting
that everyone was treated equally

but the older i get the better i know
    i'll stay on the west coast thank you
racism still shows its frayed edges
in middle america
and in every greyhound bus station
wherever i go, there it is

it's in the grandparents
and the casual conversations over dinner
and during elections
and drunken parties
and whenever
i get complimented

on how well i speak english

IO

attracted to her beauty
io had nowhere to run

meanwhile up on mt olympus
hera was getting suspicious
of her husband's absence

she went looking for him
and found him in a pasture
standing next to a beautiful heifer
hera thought it was io

but she didn't know for sure
so she asks in a sweet tone
   where did you get the heifer
   oh my husband, king of the gods?
zeus decided to play along saying

   i created it out of the ground
   well it's certainly beautiful hera said
with her hand on io's head
their eyes met and hera smiled
   give it to me as a present then
she suggested

and zeus felt cold sweat
run down his back
he couldn't hand over his mistress
who was already looking distressed
and starting to chew her cud
but hera thought it was only a heifer
he couldn't nickel and dime her

so he handed io over
crossing his fingers to save her later

argus was assigned to watch her
hera's choice couldn't have been better
this boy had a hundred eyes
he never fell asleep
zeus sent mercury to try
with stories, wine and lullabies

and when the last eye finally shut
mercury cut his head off
hera took the eyes
and gave them to her peacock
then she sent a gadfly to torment io
chased her all the way
to the mouth of the nile
where she resumed her human shape
decided to hang out in egypt awhile

until hera and zeus forgot all about her

NIGHT STALKER GOT MARRIED

the night stalker got married at san quentin
the serial killer took a wife
and called her mrs. richard ramirez

it was true love, they said
but they never got to go to bed
that's not allowed for death row inmates

she was a freelance editor
he was convicted of torture
i guess they had a lot to talk about

SEEKING SPACE ALIENS

charming her way out of trouble
doubling back on her trail
making sure she's not followed
by people thinking she was
        a piece of action

in her fantasy life
more arrogant pursuers got
their tongues cut out in dark alleys
by a knife that she carried in her coat pocket
never made the fantasy real

just felt up the handle once in a while
as she drank from her draft beer
in some smoky tavern
fielded twenty questions
drunken inquisitions

from people too nosy
to mind their own business
traveling alone, she had to be careful
always grateful to her guardian angels
constant conflict with devils

she fought the internal battle of
good versus evil on a daily basis
seeking spaces alien to her
because home didn't feel the same anymore
the image was more delicious

than when she was actually there
collecting urban myths
and personal stories
eavesdropping in coffeehouses
to support her research of

the collective unconscious
a litmus test measuring
the local decline of western civilization
accelerated to the speed of light
images captured on the television

feeding our superstitions
we carry condoms in our wallets
weapons in our pockets
to weave a spell strong enough
that we can protect ourselves

in strange places
seeking spaces alien to us
because home doesn't feel the same
anymore

TV CHILD

tv child
what was it like
before direct dial
spinning 45s
on the stereo console
watching cable
kimba the white lion and speed racer
global village vietnam
nightly news saigon
dim sum view of what's going on
who was the s.l.a. anyway
everyone was so uptight
willing to fight
for some real or imagined cause
donald defreeze died at the scene
in a shootout with the lapd
sarah jane parker
squeaky fromme
pulled out their guns
taking pot shots at the president
they got sent through
the california penal system
like charlie and sirhan sirhan
shootout in the courtroom
with angela davis
alcatraz gets taken over
by native americans
harvey milk and george moscone
get shot by a malcontent
and the sentiment sends
police cars on fire
while the zodiac killer runs loose
in blue spruce park
down the street
from my grandmother's house

BEAUTIFUL BOY

beautiful boy
seventies child
eyes opened wide
in an ecstasy smile
trance dance
trippy dippy
dizzy gillespie
with his cheeks
spread out to there
stuffed with sour lemon balls
baseball cap
bobby brady striped shirt
tribal gravy just add water
tomorrow he'll be the store clerk
behind the bodega counter
dancing on ecstasy
he ends up at a party
then head to minnie's for 24-hour fettuccini
go back to the house with some pals
watch the sun come out over the city
trading kisses getting sleepy
they start debating
who's going to get the coffee?

COFFEE POT

it all started with the coffeepot
at least that's what i thought

when she started
throwing coffee beans around

spilling water
cursing the leak

underneath the percolator
the final result

is iced coffee
weak and watery

and we discuss quietly
whether to make a fresh pot of coffee

without offending her
but she's offended already

so what do we care
so we go upstairs in search of java

we find the other coffeepot
and the coffee filters

but we can't find the coffee
and we're not asking any questions

i wouldn't do that if i were you
her boyfriend warns us

we look at each other and agree
making coffee wasn't our responsibility

or maybe it was
it doesn't matter

there's something up her ass
besides the coffee percolator

there's tension in the air upstairs
we get some sodas

share a cigarette together
it was too late for coffee anyway

DAYS IN DETOX

he's talking about his days in detox
about having to drag
a giant teddy bear
with a black sabbath t-shirt on

to discourage him
from rock and roll world
i was lucky he says
at least i didn't have to carry

the giant paper mache
crack pipe
that's what happened
when you talked about

the good old drug days
they called that glorification
disassociation by humiliation
brainwashing rituals

to make you think different
we couldn't even have sex, he tells us
family please be aware
i'm getting a cup of coffee

family is aware we all reply
family please be aware
i'm going to use the bathroom
family is aware we all reply

family please be aware
that i'm getting a second helping
of mashed potatoes
family is aware we all reply

at least, he says
i avoided getting my head shaved
and having to wear a diaper
that was called infancy

DENVER

mountains loom
at the colorado border

clarity of light calling my soul
lightness of being
one with the road
hamlet of skyscrapers

denver's domain
almost matches
purple mountains' majesty
and night meets us

in cheyenne, wyoming
for a roadside party
in the land of a million cows
there's the smell of prosperity

stench stains my clothes
past eden past loveland
past hell's half-acre
end of the world due east

where clouds meet the horizon
dying twin suns
cast a glimmer
in the evening sky

the moon laughs
as she races by
diana on the hunt
hitchhiking ghosts

flag me down
vivid hallucinations
mile marker 1300
astral projecting

into other directions
at custer's last stand
the clutch goes kablooey
and in the hills

i imagine indians laughing
    hey honey
    maybe you should have
    gotten a jeep cherokee

DOING THE DOG

in blythe we stop
for a fast food run
the bus smells like
a fat greasy french fry

one guy is missing
he comes up running
    i can tell the ride is going to be better
says the driver to the stranger

    i can tell because you've been smoking marijuana
    i could smell it when you walked by
the passenger tries to deny
a little old lady catcalls him

    maybe next time you'll be on time
the guy across the aisle
is drinking from
a cough medicine bottle

and the bathroom smells like bad gas
the folks trapped in the back
bemoan their fate
razz the perpetrator

    hey man, what did you have for dinner?
    hey man, close the door, it stinks
    hey man, why didn't you go stink up mcdonald's
        when you had the chance?

EAST COAST STORY

east coast story
of a happy go lucky family

that broke up badly
a bitter custody battle ensued

but before the courts could choose
the husband the father the man

he really lost it
he ties his wife up to a chair

makes her write out a will
she escapes

runs next door
calls the police

but before they could get there
he already killed their

two-year-old daughter
by stuffing her in a plastic bag

he shoots himself dead
with a gun to the head

while the little boy
maybe four

is sitting on the porch
telling the neighbors how

his father put sister
in the garbage

WALKING IN THE MOONLIGHT

walking in the moonlight
of a mexican beach
old man watching the tide
waves lapping slowly

    gather round little children
    while i tell you a story
    moon as my witness
    we were staying at a secluded beach house
    miles out of town
    we didn't hear the warnings
    of a hurricane approaching
    the waves grew violent
    wind whistled through the jungle
    we started to realize
    we were in trouble
    barricaded windows and doors
    caught unprepared
    we couldn't do much more
    but wait in the kitchen
    for the uninvited guest
    water began pouring in the house
    we tied ourselves to the kitchen counter
    while hell was breaking loose
    dishes flying into space
    frying pan hit me in the head
    almost knocking me cold
    alive with fright
    adrenaline rush
    hold the rope tight
    while ocean water
    swirled around our waists
    suddenly everything was still
    deafening quiet
    eye of the storm

nothing quite like it
tempest in a teacup
all the water made it hard to breathe
much less scream
and looking down
i saw fish
swimming on the kitchen floor

SPOKANE

limping to spokane in second gear
missing some gear teeth
can't go any faster than
25 miles per hour
white light and holy water can't undo
the evil done
another in a long line of bad carma
wreaking havoc on electrical systems
graduated to another kind of car tramua
gears and transmissions
days later still stuck in spokane
waiting for parts from other lands
make a list of things to sell,
things to take
survival in action my reaction
sit and cry i can't
it's a kamikaze mission
chevron station my second home
roam in the riverpark
watch the water
nice people nice places
the femme next to me
a little too nice
i let her buy me rum and cokes
we talk and joke
about the time
her husband caught her in bed
with another woman
strange dreams hang from the garage ceiling
along with the chains and pulleys
make peace with the jeep
sleeping bag in the back seat
beat it with flowers and latin phrases
e pluribus unum
dreams of chrysler
and biting the ear off lee iacocca

OLYMPIA

headachy from cigarettes
try to recapture the day's events
left the house for a cup of latte
ended up at an all day party
sitting on the porch
bumming a smoke
reading the rag
suddenly this guy next to me asks
    what is this jaw?
fox jaw always good for conversation
small talk about my trip, my transmission
    hey, he says, i know where there's a
    really good band playing
    past deschutes, past little rock
    wrong turn at the driving range
    past the abandoned store
    up the road two miles
    rainbow valley, traveler's haven
    you know you're there when you see
    people picking strawberries
    and hear the band playing

MISSED CONNECTIONS

thinking of you
wondering where you went
and that time we almost met
one night in san francisco

i got the message late
to meet you at the mermen show
i heard you got really drunk
i heard you broke a lot of stuff

i heard you even threw up
and that you were
falling down a sidewalk so bad
a passing hooker had to pick you up

i heard you didn't want to go inside
because i might be there
i heard you were staying
on divisidero street

but no one has seen you

ROAD TO FLAGSTAFF

he's reclined in the back of the pickup
a painter in repose
but his body is more like a model's
he's so sensual lying there
between the mountain bike
and the spare tire
the 12-pack of milwaukee's best
and the computer

i think he's crushing
the saltine crackers
he asks me to kiss him
and i decline without a good reason
cover him with my jacket
watch him sleeping
wonder what his lips feel like
wonder what i'm missing

SOUNDMAN

he was a soundman for a touring band
one night in jersey
the show ended early so
he took off to the beach
with the guitarist named jerry
and two girls they met that night

one couple disappeared
heading for the pier
while the other couple walked hand in hand
to the ocean's edge
they started to make out
things got hot, clothes came off
making love like it was 'here to eternity'

then he tells me
    that's not even the story
    it goes like this
        afterwards we were at the breakwater wall
        left all our stuff on the beach
        and in the middle of sharing a deep soul kiss
        she looks over my shoulder
        and breaking free she screams ohmigod
        and turning around i could see
        all our stuff just floating away
        bobbing on the ocean waves
        she lost her purse but i think
        i had it worse - all i could find
        were my shoes
        she had a dirty t-shirt i could use
        but that was it
        i caught so much shit from the band
        the next day
        and she wasn't even my type

WITH A VIDEO CAMERA

with a video camera
he would tape bands in bars
get knocked down by guitarists

while trying to get the weird angles
of the crazy dancing frontman
his goal in life was to be

seattle correspondent for mtv
in the deli, he tries to make
the store clerk smile

hands him a flyer saying
   watch dave's dimension!
   cable access television

   channel 23!
he was newly returned
from a european vacation

working on street corners
as a musician
spare change and a little attention

crazy american
with a saxophone
should have known

his type of lifestyle
would get sociopathic after awhile
it drove one girlfriend
to run him over
she's still doing time
for attempted murder

MOTHER OF FOUR

mother of four
twenty-two years old

had a hard day at work
her boss was a jerk

the customers were worse
taking a coffeebreak

before going home to see
what kind of trouble

the kids got into
she walks into denny's

which is usually friendly
but the next table over

started complaining
about her cigarette smoke

they weren't even nice about it
they were rude and uptight about it

she finally broke
she goes home

not saying a word to anyone
the kids wondered what they had done

she picks up the 12-gauge shotgun
takes it back to the restaurant

shot one complainer dead
in the parking lot

you know
she said when the cops

finally found her
    i've had it

    up to here
    with these goddamn non-smokers

WAITING GAME

digging up bones
to make way for the living

pink stucco apartment buildings
and two more lanes of freeway

the living get greedy for real estate
mountain views in the foothills

everyone has a price
it becomes a waiting game

for the right descendents to come along
they eventually show up

even if it takes a generation or two
the buyers can afford to wait

wanderlust calls the children
some things you have to see for yourself

even if you know the good life
has been there all along

sometimes you don't go back
paradise is overrated

SHOTGUN WEDDING

if i wanted my life any harder
   she tells me
i'd let my old man know
where he could find me

it was a shotgun wedding naturally
you think i wanted to marry
that son of a bitch?
first you know nothing of my life

my dad died when i was 10
my mother soon after
i was drinking by the time i was 12
one night at a party

i got drunk and woke up
with this guy on top of me
i was missing my clothes
i got really cold

pushed him off me
to this day i couldn't tell you
if i lost my virginity
a couple of years later

i got together with jed's father
he was such an asshole
but he took care of me
so when i got pregnant

we got married

HE STRANGLED HIS GIRLFRIEND

he strangled his girlfriend
and headed to alaska
to hide out awhile
until the fury died down

he stayed with a buddy
but things got funny
things got pretty bad
one night while watching tv

his picture flashes on the screen
it was one of those cop shows
scramble for the remote control
before anyone walked into the room

but it didn't matter
someone called the number
the tattoo of the skull
getting its brains blown out

was a dead giveaway

THE THIEF WAS KIND

the thief was kind
in his own special way
as if to say

    if this had been
    someone else honey
    all your shit would be gone

coming back from canal street
you could tell someone
fucked with the jeep

he took my clothes and my shoes
but he left my makeup
i guess he couldn't use it

he took my fix-a-flat
but he left my black fur hat
he took my favorite t-shirt

but he left my jacket
which was filthy
and i was kind of grateful

the thief was being so picky
he took my curling iron
but he left my tape

of the best of earth, wind and fire
he took all my books
except for the guide

to free campgrounds
he wanted to stick around the city
i know this because he took

my map of new orleans
he took my wallet
some ids some keys

but the motherfucker
left the rock
that he used to break in with

TREASURE ISLAND

panhandling the bar
to bail her cat out of jail

he wasn't a bad cat
just a calico in the habit

of hanging out at a hotel
where they finally called the cops

i tried to warn him, she said
but he wouldn't listen
and now treasure island

was doing time
until she could come up

with the money
for the $80 fine

SIDEWALK PHILOSOPHIES

hey man spare a buck
down on my luck
can you help me out
got a cigarette? how about a light?
how about a coffee?
i can go for some caffeine
don't you have anything at all?

and it's the story all over
the country is torn asunder
no one understands each other
split between the needy and the greedy
and an imbalance in the economy
with a heaping dose
of paranoia

television is teaching us
to fear the stranger
the family member, the preacher
the guy behind the meat counter
the ex-spouse or the ex-lover
the ex-friend who felt fucked over
people close to the edge

and we eat it up
hold up let me get my videocamera
in case something happens
maybe i can sell it to the highest bidder
television is the opiate of the masses
cannibal cop shows console us
showing us people are worse off

capitalism depends on
keeping someone down
as long as it isn't me
make it someone else not me
every time the unemployment rates drop
the dow jones takes a plunge
over concerns of rising interest

the ensuing economic formula is
people working is bad for business
as american athletic shoe companies
are posting record earnings
on the backs of pakistanis
one president had this saying
that the business of america is business

and that became the accepted platitude
big business got greedy
the trickle down theory
is a fairytale from the eighties
it doesn't exist in reality
and the business of america
is people

SEATTLE SUN

he was on his way
to join a coven of white witches
when he ran into a group

of discontented college graduates
heading northeast
to raise a little hell

he packed up his powerbook
and went along
though his scars ran deep

and never healed properly
in the seattle sun
he drank lots of black coffee

NOC NOC CLUB

noc noc club

lower haight
keith haring
tribal style

this place is great
let's move on
when you get content

there's something wrong
brave new world
our second home

soul sister bartender
inherited the bar
from her father

installing a new sound system
so the broun fellinis
can play in the back

young jazz cats
getting high dressed in black
and drinking irish coffees

ON THE SEVENTH HOUR

on the seventh hour
of the seventh day
of the seventh month
the fireworks go off in pamplona

at the bottom of the hill
the bulls get anxious in the corral
until it breaks and they escape
running towards the waiting crowd

i was never as drunk
in all my life
   he said
as i was my first night in spain

running with the bulls
it's amazing how fast you can move
when you look behind
and unless you're facing death

the spectators will throw you back
to finish the race to the arena
so you can wear that red bandana
be a hero for the day

PRACTICING SWORD MOVES

practicing sword moves
in the living room

raven curls pinned back
in a red velvet cape

and stainless steel
vegetable steamers

taped to her tits
her favorite game

with boyfriends
was dominance and discipline

   and you know what
she tells me

   i just got the soundtrack
   to conan the barbarian

THE RED DRESS

for years her neighbors suspected

dark secrets hidden
by false smiles

for years she masked it
and everyone played along

like a sick and twisted joke
smiling supermarket clerk

always explaining her bruises
as due to her clumsiness

always smiling
one day her husband died suddenly

as fast as a car accident or a heart attack
at the funeral

she didn't wear black
she shed her martyr syndrome

in a moment of bravado
and showed up to the burial

wearing a red sequin party dress
that came down to her ankles

they put the coffin in the grave
she threw in her wedding ring

gave a strange laugh shouting
    i hope you're happy now, lawrence

i hope you're happy now
because i certainly am!

and all the women silently cheered her on
red dress and all

while all the men wondered
what their funerals would be like

PEEP SHOW PRINCESS

she lies on a dirty shag carpet
and flirts with men
through the plate glass window

dancing girl
would show them her secret places
wearing a long black wig

lips parted in false invitation
in exchange for tattered sexy bills
her boyfriends think it's sexy

it's one of those things
that attracted them in the first place
her boyfriends let her do anything she wanted

and what she wanted mostly
was hanging out with her ex-boyfriends
she would walk down central avenue

in a short dress and no underwear
so when the wind gusted
you could see all of her

she would walk around the house
in a thong bikini
drip drying her g-strings in the living room

so the eyes of my friends can pop out
and i have to stop, pick them up
put them back in

so they can stare better
when she comes back in a short dress
and sits cross-legged

still in no underwear
dancing girl could change her moods
as fast as she could change her wig

turning from temperamental primadonna
to self-righteous sex kitten
to college student hiding her secret

behind black horn-rimmed glasses
shouting   i'm the bad guy, i'm the bad guy!
dancing girl

had her windshield broken
by random vandalism
she got a great deal on a replacement

from an auto salvage clerk
who admires her occupation
dancing girl

hoped her family never found out
especially her brother
no matter how liberal minded

there would still be a scandal
and if her mother found out
that she had raised a stripper

she never would have helped pay
for college tuition

ONE WEEK

on Sunday she moved out of the house

amidst a nasty cat fight
on Monday her favorite uncle died of cancer

on Tuesday her boyfriend seemed to disappear
and a close friend thought she found a tumor

on Wednesday her cousin shot his wife
in the driveway then himself

with all the kids watching
she couldn't remember what happened Thursday

on Friday she started looking for her boyfriend
the way he was nowhere got her attention

ONE SUMMER

one summer
she left
all her plans
her cool jobs
her school
her sunlit bedroom
in noe noe land
for a bus ride
to guatemala
her lover went along
but something went wrong
she still cries
to tell the story
      we had a really bad fight
      no holds barred
      we said a lot of things
      in anger
      the next day
      still not speaking
      he went out in his kayak
      but he never came back
      he drowned in the rapids
      i really lost it
      they put me on a plane
      in guatemala city
      three days on the bus
      with his body behind me
      i went a little crazy
      but the prozac really helps

OAKLAND BUS STATION

morning commuters at the bart station
in their dark blues, grays and blacks

same colors as the neighborhood guys
but a completely different look

knit caps, old english on the back spells "dog"
black sweatshirts, chino pants in any basic color

vinyl jacket, flair jeans frayed to the ankle
black demon chevrolet super clean 4-door lumina

speeds across the greyhound parking lot
black rosary hanging from the rearview window

waves of overcast clouds start breaking up
it's going to be a beautiful day

speeding down the freeway
weaving through the traffic, tailgating semis

passing a joint in a golden circle
as cypress hill blares from the stereo

getting high on the way to bayfair
out of the way because there's too much 5-0

at the oakland station
stopping to do a line

but running out of time
and a wave of paranoia

cutting on cassette covers
with a ginsu knife in its homemade sheath

only mexicans carry knives, they laugh
swapping tales of the fights they recently got into

exchanging gossip about the people in town
people in jail, and the girls they used to go out with

students of urban survival, old school homies
making a living dealing crank

out of little plastic baggies
bickering over who owes what

nickel and diming like a rendition of
    who's on first, what's on second

and they played with the knives
like they might have played with their toys

brown boys eyes glittering from the rail
just inhaled in a bart station parking lot

another car drives up, maroon monte carlo
security guy stands nearby during the reunion

not inclined to stick around
for a second round of killer

i say my thank yous and good-bye kisses
catch the train to san francisco

NEWSROOM

always showing up for work
deep mysteries hidden within

copy editor with a crack addiction
his mother made the best finger sandwiches

the photographer with a drinking problem
the assistant managing editor with control issues

the efficient people hater who never shuts up
the editor runs columns predicting

dow hitting 15,000 by the end of the century
corporate likes what it hears

and the editor is promoted to the land of gated communities
and backyard golf courses

he writes weekly columns through the world view
of his neighbors and focus groups

the newsroom is on war alert
get the names of local soldiers

get the reaction of local people
send the interns to the supermarkets

to troll the aisles, take a photographer
    can i interview you for the newspaper?

the television is on
the television will announce the beginning

of the bombing
at any moment

IF I WERE A MAN

if i were a man
i'd be a drag queen

sight unseen
in satin and leather

silk and chiffon
depending on whether

it was dancing or dinner
long black hair

down to there
six-inch stiletto heels

the kind that make an imprint
when walking on a stranger's back

a set of fake tits
the kind that really fit

and look real
friends invited to feel

underneath my sequin dresses
hanging out at the bar

no action so far
    don't talk to me now   she says

    can't you see
    i'm cruising?

GATHERING OF MAMMALS

gathering of mammals
dancing in the dust

young beauties
weird nerdies

dressed like peacocks and ravens
cigarette machine

eats a dollar
go the beer garden

and holler to get her money back
hanging out with madcaps

who sing a cappella
at the drop of a hat

renditions for an audience of one
still looking for cigarettes

nicotine drug dealer
out right now

check back later
walk a mile for a camel

and a cup of latte
kids playing ball behind the deli

old man looking for cans in the alley
shy smiles of strangers

GIRLFIGHT

bad shit going down
in the parking lot behind safeway
young girls waiting for their prey
adolescent confrontation

yeah i heard you were after my man
yeah that's right he told me
whatcha got to say to that, bitch?
she got it all wrong

the intended victim moves on
starts to walk away
gets jumped anyway
and the punches fly wild

kicking and scratching
and the cursing
    filipina chola wannabe ho
biting and slapping

    ugly spic mad dog bitch
beating each other's heads
on the pavement
blood on the cement

getting pulled away
to the crowd's dismay
they go home
nurse their wounds

and get the story ready
ready to act chummy
for the next day's meeting
with the assistant vice-principal

LOCAL DRUGSTORE

i have uppers downers
a bit of really kind bud
       she told me
i have a soup from the
local coffeehouse
i have a phone number
of where to get coke
but i don't have any tylenol

HEROIN HOUSE

let's all go to the heroin house
the heroin house
the heroin house
let's all go to the heroin house
and shoot up some smack

actually he couldn't wait
we drive up the corner
of fifth and bonnie
and before we even stop
these guys run out
and he's asking
    do you have any chiva?
they pull little balloons
out of their mouths
he buys four, we drive off
we weren't there for more than a minute
we go find a pay phone
and a public restroom
land in a mexican restaurant
he knows we're in a hurry
starts to worry about the smells of
burning heroin
that everyone would know
so he breaks the needle off the syringe
and puts it up his nose
we tumble back
to the rented town-car
    thanks
he says
    i feel a lot better now

HE WAS A GOOD KID

he was a good kid
until he started stealing

finally culminating
in a credit card shopping spree

plastic fantasy
his mother freaked when

she got the bill
his father held him down

with his pants around his ankles
while his mother beat his ass

with a baseball bat
he never forgot that

he said later
it was self defense

the next time
he and his mom

got into an argument
but he took that same baseball bat

gave his mother forty whacks
hit her so hard the bat broke

his father found her
when he came home

LOCKED IN A CEMETERY

locked in a cemetery
on a lonely christmas night

daughters of darkness
didn't want to stay

just visit awhile
and take pictures of each other

standing next to tombstones
in thigh-high snow

she was missing her kid
hating her life

opening doors to other sides
or pretending to

was stupid fun diversion
for a boring christmas night

climbing the ironrod fence
    was sure a bitch

she said
    my friend got stuck

    i had to get a passing drunk
    to help me boost her over

KING OF GOLDEN GATE PARK

the king of golden gate park
has his couriers
keep an eye out for the cops
while smoking some reefer

dug up in the roots
of a nearby eucalyptus
i got five grand sunk in the haight
lent out to people

who live on the street
i guess i don't have to tell you
what i do for a living, he tells me
it's a person's obligation

to fight laws that are unjust
the people that are passing the laws
aren't passing them for us
it's not about marijuana

or about adults smoking flowers
it's a money thing
because the fines
and seized property brings

revenue to the city
and the law enforcement agencies
so the marijuana laws
aren't there to serve people

they're there to make us all criminals

IT STARTS

innocently enough, it starts
trigger a sense of moral outrage
ask questions with uncomfortable answers
flashbacks of bad decisions

never thought the roosters would come home
the karmic wheel turns
children born of fear
and fed fast food culture

but not much nutrition
you will be sold milk that makes
daughters bleed early
pharmaceutical companies

will develop a pill to combat it
you will purchase that as well
dominant culture seeps into unconscious
birth school work death

caught in the fifty-year plans of corporate cultures
substituting gold for god
blood of Christ is sold by the spoonful
the motive is to make money by the handful

some say
you can't be too rich or too beautiful
go under the knife
for a few moments in the spotlight

INTERNATIONAL SCOUT

surly midget clerk
at the 7-11

sun's still out by the time
we reach rosalyn

outside the town
there's a dry lakebed

ground looking pretty solid
go four-wheeling on it

get stuck in the middle
a dry lakebed, a forest of tree stumps

without even a shovel
dave takes a bicycle

to get some help
leaving us two

in the mud
in the sun

by ourselves
left to dig the scout out

covered in mud
getting hot

laughing kissing
making out

by the rear left tire
after a while

stop to actually dig
the tire out

drive the scout
from the lake bed

go look for david
get a pizza

and find a campground

IN THE MISSION

in the mission
the sun always shines

and crack dealers
hang out at the end of my block

with any luck
they ignore you

when you walk by
at 2 a.m. there are

congas in the basement
and a junkie in the kitchen

looking for clean needles
while the offbeat

bonk bonk bonk
filters up the stairs

the other day
these homeless guys

wandered by
with time to kill

new found pals
singing corridos

in the hall
he got his guitar to join them

but when he wasn't looking
they disappeared with his six-string

in his anguish
he broke the windshield

of a passing car
got hauled off to jail

while at home
his crazy italian girlfriend

would pick fights
with the housemates

two years in the country
and she still didn't know any english

PERSONAL HISTORY

west coast home
california bred
new mexico born
not chicano or puerto ricano
and certainly not hissss-panic
some say spanish
but that's not quite accurate
erasing the mestizo
call me a norteno

bloodlines here long before
pilgrim's pride manifest destiny
families escaping with their lives
from torquemada's questioning
spreading religion among indigenous people
to create its own iconography
altar building a specialty
overtly catholic
covertly jewish

double whammy guilt complex
that still makes it hard
for some norteno kids
to come out of the closet
speaking hybrid spanglish
spanish was the secret language
used by adults
to talk about the war
where my father was

to talk about the bills
to talk about stuff
i still don't know what
wasn't paying much attention
watched a lot of cable television

quality time with my grandfather
who sat perched on his barcalounger
sometimes building furniture
for my barbies to hang out on

busy spinning my mother's records
on my little suitcase turntable
bounded by the beatles
little green apple
hey jude on one side
revolution on the other
it's a point of pride for most nortenos
to serve the country in a time of war
inferiority complex about being americans

makes them feel as if they got
something to prove
a reliable unit to send into combat
easily draftable, not college exemptible
going to canada never an option
too much pride to risk being called a coward
disproportionately high number of body bags
awarded the medal of valor
a cross erected in every village

ACKNOWLEDGMENTS

Most of these poems originally appeared in the chapbooks *Devil in a Blue Dress, Spirit of the Stairs, He Strangled His Girlfriend and Other Tales from the Road, Orchestra of Harpies, Wicked, Cannibals of North America, Misfit Clique,* and *The Night Stalker Got Married.* Individual pieces also appeared in *Flipside, Kink, Conceptions Southwest, Calyx, Manila, The Temple, Poetry Slam: The Competitive Art of Performance Poetry, Carp.*

James Tracy, Jen Joseph, Jon Longhi and Bucky Sinister: thank you for being so solid. Thanks goes out to the folks at Last Gasp, Taos Poetry Circus, City Lights bookstore, Modern Times bookstore, Top Shelf Comics, Lollapalooza/Larrikin Management, and the design production departments at the *Weekly Alibi, Albuquerque Tribune, The Stranger, Anchorage Daily News,* and the *Albuquerque Journal.* Love and thanks to the following people: Mark Ryden, Sherman Alexie, John Nichols, KRK Ryden, Bob Holman, Robert Masterson, Fran Maher, Brad Beshaw, Nikki and Ted Gardner, Stuart Ross, Noel Franklin, Paul Rueckhaus, Judith Roche, Adam Parfrey, Hannah Tashjian, Chloe Eudaly, Dayvid Figler, Wammo, Phil West, Mike Henry, Rafael Alvarado, Rudy Carrillo, Jon Little, Hank Stuever, KayLynn Deveney, Anita Baca, Bob Benz & Lara Edge, David Fischer, Hank Hyena, Victor Infante, Lisa Verlo, Mitch and Donna Rayes, Lisa Gill, Karla Esquivel, Julie Serna, Pleasant Gehman, S.A. Griffin, Iris Berry, and Kevin Sampsell and Powell's Bookstore. And finally, I need to thank all the folks involved in my art project, Kapow! Ivan Brunetti, Sam Henderson, Steve Weissman, Jordan Crane, Shappy, Kristen Casselman, Lloyd Dangle, Josh Berkowitz, Janelle Hessig, David Choe, Beau Sia, Cristin O'Keefe Aptowicz, Jaime Crespo, George Tirado, Gabby Gamboa, Ron Rege, Rafael Navarro, Eric Reynolds, Greg Zura, James Kochalka, Mats, Keith Knight, Cas McGee, Kurt Wolfgang, Pete Sickman-Garner, Johnny Ryan, Chelsea Starr, Kenn Rodriguez, Matthew John Conley, Tarin Towers. In Memoriam: Helen Mondragon and Michael Salazar.

ABOUT THE AUTHOR

Juliette Torrez's writing has appeared in a wide variety of publications including *Sic Vice and Verse*, *Kink*, *Calyx*, and on the website About.com. She is the publisher of Kapow!, a critically acclaimed, award-winning press that unites cutting-edge comix art with contemporary poetry in a zine format touting high production values. Torrez has been an active organizer in the national spoken word community through her work with the Lollapalooza Festival, the National Poetry Slam, Taos Poetry Circus, and the Albuquerque Poetry Festival. Her early ezine/blog *Poetry Channel and Information Network* was instrumental in building a national touring circuit for spoken word artists. She wrote and edited *The Sofasurfing Handbook: A Guide for Modern Nomads* (Manic D Press) and co-edited *Revival: Spoken Word from Lollapalooza 94* (Manic D Press). Named among the "Outstanding Women of America" while attending University of New Mexico, she received awards from the Society of Newspaper Design during her tenure at the *Albuquerque Journal*. Juliette Torrez currently lives in San Francisco.